Meet me under the same moon

Jose Guillermo (William) Maldonado Pena

Written and arranged by
Jose Guillermo (William) Maldonado Pena

This book is dedicated to the one rose,
who smiled a bright and warming smile
towards my direction.
Not only lighting up a man, but a soul as well.
I will refer to her as my rose, my moon, my light, and anything beautiful
that you could think of.

So, for now in written words, I want to thank you.

Thank you!
.

I really do hope that you and everybody else
who manages to get a copy enjoy reading some of my writing
and that it touches your soul as it does mine.
...
...
so please,
enjoy and happy reading.

Follow me on Instagram: *@jose.williamm*

Follow me on Snapchat: *@jmaldonado9u*

Follow my Facebook page: *@Jose William M*

Meet me under the same moon

A series of poems about love.

By

Jose Guillermo (William) Maldonado Pena

-J. William-
Meet me under the same moon

There is something
that is always on the back of my mind.
Does she ever think about me
during the day or at night?
Does she ever wonder
what the heck am I doing
on a Sunday morning?
Does she ever wonder who I'm with?
Does it even cross her mind
if I'm happy or sad?

I really don't know,

but I just want you to know,
I sure do think about you all the time,
that's why every day,
there is a different poem about you,
and you just happen to always
be the muse to each piece,
and for that I Thank You.

I am homesick for a place
that I'm not sure even exists.
One where my heart feels full.
One where judgement has no effect
on the way I were to see myself.
A place where my body, mind,
and soul is understood.
I had it once,
but it slowly slipped away from my fingertips.
Now I long for that feeling once more.
To rest, to sleep, and to feel whole again
in between someone's arms.

-J. William-
Meet me under the same moon

So, you are still
on my unfinished thoughts.
A day passes by,
A month passes by,
A year passes by.
Then after a tiny blur
of confusion and getting lost.

The story continues,
with a little pause.

It is a very rare, enlightening, and
fortunate phenomenon.
To find someone who
can make you feel like your
insanity and your chaos,
be completely logical and in order.
And somehow you manage to do all that
with just a picture and a smile.

I want the honest truth
about your love.
Like the silver tie which binds
the sun and moon,
the heart to heart,
the mind to mind
in body and in soul.
This silver link that binds us
to the universe.
I want to know the truth,
does it exist between
you and I?
Does it bind us together like
I and you or in sun and you or
in moon and I?
Does it even exist in your thoughts?
I just want to know
the honest truth about our love.

Speak the words you want to hear
from the deepest part of my soul.
Are they
Sun, moon, and stars
or are they
heart, mind, and soul
or are they
Poetry, flowers, and life?
Show me, what are the desired words
you want to hear from the voice of my soul.
Show me, what words will make you
want to spend your precious time on me.
Could it possibly be the word,
"Love".

Inside my chest,
the heartbeat within will always
remain calm and steady,
but the loneliness within
remains superior to love.
Which sleeps very softly and
lies in secrecy,
but get close
and your ears
shall hear very faintly the thumps and desires
for your love one after the other.

-J. William-
Meet me under the same moon

Use me...
Use me as an instrument
to bring your soul alive.
Let my melody
pinch your soul,
just so that it wakes up;
and it starts to dance under our
beautiful blue moon.

-J. William-
Meet me under the same moon

As I stare into the sky's ocean
of infinite stars.
Each one of those stars containing
countless worlds like ours,
and like theirs, ours are also boundless
and never ending in miracle making,
and compared to the vastness of the world
or the universe in fact,
man's existence in this world
is very insignificant and the things
that us insignificant humans fret about
are petty indeed, but what do I know,
I'm just staring at the sparkling glitter
in the sky.

A man who is honest,
pure, and true.
Yields his soul captive
to intoxicating love,
but he cannot keep it to himself.
He must spend it.
He must give it away.
Who here has the courage
to release him
from the love chains that hold
his soul captive and imprisoned?

-J. William-
Meet me under the same moon

I wish to see into your eyes.
Imagine the wonders that
I would see.
To picture the world as only you do.

I want to see the sorrow and the sadness
that you and only you can bare alone.
I want to see and face the demons
and the shadows that hide behind
that beautiful smile of yours.
Show me the unseen burdens you carry
around your shoulders every day.
The ones I get to glimpse in your eyes
when you think I'm not looking.

I guess what I'm really trying to tell you
is that,
I just want to understand the
"YOU" which you hide from
everyone else.

-J. William-
Meet me under the same moon

You may not have
much to say
but in the dark,
I can hear
your silent whispers.
Very deep and
very hidden.
Screaming and echoing
the wish for some type
of love.

-J. William-
Meet me under the same moon

Just the thought of a
conversation between
yourself and I.
Makes the breathing in my chest
and my heart pump
a hundred times faster.
All while having butterflies
in my stomach,
while mumbling
a hundred words a second.
Imagine having a
conversation in real life
with your beautiful soul.
Now that would be beautiful,
but also, very chaotic.

-J. William-
Meet me under the same moon

There is this feeling
that is slowly
creeping up on me.
A feeling of fear of
never knowing exactly how to
uncurl my fingertips.
Gently giving you back
to this universe we all
come from.

-J. William-
Meet me under the same moon

For the beauty
that you are.
It is madness to hate
all what is the rose.
Yes, indeed the beautiful
corolla remains an
untouchable illusion,
but even poisoned thorns
need watering every
now and then.

-J. William-
Meet me under the same moon

22

My soul and I
hope to find your love
in many other
lifetimes to come,
because one
is not enough
to show,
to give you all my love.

-J. William-
Meet me under the same moon

Your smile,
a fountain
of divine light.
Making everybody
in its vicinity to freshen
up their loving hearts.
While I remain waiting
for my turn to come.

The moon when
leaning over such
a beautiful rose flower
makes the wrinkles
of my heart more indelible,
than those of the ripples
that are created from the
fountain that you
drink from.

-J. William-
Meet me under the same moon

Share your love, share your life
and expand yourself in greater depth.
Connect with your heart and explore the universe
that you hide within.
We are so lucky to be alive, but still
our lives are nothing but a cosmic blink.
Even our seemingly all-encompassing world
is but a tiny blue dot, circling around an average size star.
Spiraling around a galaxy of four hundred billion stars,
which in itself is just one galaxy amongst billions more
and for a brief moment we get to experience the wonders
of existence, of consciousness, and awareness.
To experience emotions like love and sadness or
beautiful experiences like meeting
the one you love for the very first time.

-J. William-
Meet me under the same moon

*Light is both the symbol
of love and truth.*

*I guess that is why I
fell hard for you.*

*You carry within,
the light of the silent sun
and the quiet moon.*

*Both which bring out the
shadows within me.
Right down to the darkest part
of my soul.*

-J. William-
Meet me under the same moon

*You soar across
the thoughts of my soul
like a beautiful
galactic star
made into forever.
A never-ending light
spinning circles around
a dark filled sky.*

*"Make a wish on her"
I did, I do
every night and every day,
for you to never fly
so far away.
That you leave
this universe of mine
and go onto the next.*

Sun and moon,
such beautiful poetry.
Earth and life,
such beautiful poetry.
Light and love,
such beautiful poetry.
The universe is everywhere
and to me there is a universe
within you.
That is why,
I use you
as my beautiful muse to make
beautiful poetry.

Darling you are a star.
A star surrounded by many
But still very alone.
I know you are sad
so, I won't tell you
"Have a good day.''
Instead I advise you too simply
"Have a day".
Keep faking that smile,
tell everybody you're happy,
wear comfortable clothes,
say whatever you want, but
please don't give up on yourself just yet.
It will be better soon, until then

"Have a day."

-J. William-
Meet me under the same moon

All within a blink of an eye,
we met before.
Afraid and shy
all I did was say hello.
Physically we have yet to touch,
but universally
the hearts of our soul
have been already connected through
a simple hello.
They have created a spiritual relationship
with each other's divine self.
A nonstop communication,
just like our sun and our moon
but still,
you and I are very much, yet to touch.

-

-J. William-
Meet me under the same moon

Watching those
morning rays
kiss such a beautiful soul.
Mesmerized by
those eyes
and that smile.
I can't help but stare and
dream that I might be
falling in love
with an angel.

-J. William-
Meet me under the same moon

I finally opened my eyes to witness
a beautiful blue moon in the sky
surrounded by darkness,
and as the wind begins to blow peacefully,
I begin to hear these
angelic whispers in the air.
There is this loudness to these whispers.
Whispers shouldn't be this loud,
should they?
What is this light?
Who is this girl, this beautiful angel?
I think she is the one calling my name.
Are you, the one calling my name?

-J. William-
Meet me under the same moon

As you stare at your body in the mirror.
You looking at you and me staring
at your reflection.
I don't just see a pretty face.
I see the most kind hearted, crazy,
compassionate, outgoing, weird,
gentle yet so strong,
and the most
independent woman that I have ever met.
Everything so deep, so hidden,
so beautiful and gorgeously trapped
within your heart that I just hope,
your soul sees that within yourself
as you begin to stare at her imperfections.

-J. William-
Meet me under the same moon

She is not only a word.
She is not only a fear.
She is not just a wave or a sea.
She is not only a beautiful butterfly
with wings of courage.
She is not only clouds and rain,
lightning and thunder.
She is not just a star in a dark sky
sprinkled with twinkling stardust.
And she will never settle for anything less.
She is Her. She is Everything. She is the light.
She Exist.
I swear to you,
She is a Universe.

A true man
is a creative lover, supporter, and caregiver.
Not just to the one person he loves
but to everybody
who he manages to touch hearts with.
Second, he must train his passions
to serve at his will.
He must
enjoy all what is beautiful,
love all what is the truth,
hate all what is the wrong, and
love all what is charity and nobly respect
the everybody and everything
around and within himself,
but first the mind of the man
must be a ready servant for the man's body
to act upon such actions.
If not trained properly,
he is but a child in a man's body.

-J. William-
Meet me under the same moon

The Earth and
The Moon and
The Sun and
The Stars
Speak through you
Awkwardly
yet beautifully.
Would you
allow me to do the
same.

-J. William-
Meet me under the same moon

The first place
we tend to lose the battle
is in our own thinking,
So please tell me,
why do I keep wanting
to go to war with the thought
that I could possibly
be something to you,
knowing that I will lose
absolutely
every single battle.

-J. William-
Meet me under the same moon

I really don't want us to end
but we never really started.
You were a cloud I was so
desperate to reach out and grab,
but never really found the core
to your strange, untouchable, and
beautiful soul.
The wind kept blowing you away from me
and now you have found
another substance to fill
that emptiness you hide within,
and I'm left wondering
will my broken heart and soul ever
get the chance to witness your rain
once again.

Meet me under the same moon

I got tremendous
Love
for those who dream
of long kisses
under the same
star filled moon.

-J. William-
Meet me under the same moon

This memory I carry within
as it starts to fade away.
Time somehow manages
to remind me of your presence,
and the sad and beautiful truth is that
as long as we have time,
understanding and silencing
this loud mind,
carrying such beautiful memories of you,
will never fade away,
because like time it shall and will
continue to remain
eternal, beautiful, and infinite.

-J. William-
Meet me under the same moon

There is no shame in crying,
for a tear is but a drop
of the spiritual ocean
seeking for acceptance.
A salty stream
mirroring emotions
that gently move from the love
that comes from the center of your soul;
and all I want right now
is to bathe in all its honesty.

-J. William-
Meet me under the same moon

You are very beautiful,
and no man would ever be able
to resist your mysterious smile.

Watching you gaze at the moon
and its beautiful and infinite light.
Wishing I could meet you there,
I dress these words of mine
to try and grasp your attention.
Cologne with flowered rose intentions.
To hopefully entice your very senses,

But I guess that thru your eyes of elegance.
My eminent soul is not worthy-of,
to be in your presence.

-J. William-
Meet me under the same moon

The ocean of storms and chaos,
comfort, peace, tranquility, and strength
you hold in your eyes
are something,
not even the strongest of people
are able to handle and mold.

-J. William-
Meet me under the same moon
(for my beautiful grandmother, may you rest in peace.)

June's love
has come around and I remember
all your hurt and pain,
but still remaining strong and fighting.
Your compassion, your heart, your wisdom,
all soothing to this dumb heart of mine.
Protecting, loving, and preventing this
family from falling apart.

Reminiscing on
your last thoughts,
on your last tears,
on your last words of goodbyes.
Wishing you were still here.
I know all beautiful angels
belong in heaven,
but why
were you taken so unexpectedly?

-J. William-
Meet me under the same moon

Look at you, I could almost
mistake you for a flower.
Grounded,
but still standing tall and beautiful
like the tallest of towers.

Filled with hopes and dreams.
Strong and sturdy,
ready to fight any type of treacherous winds,
but still remaining beautiful, kind,
compassionate, gentle, and fragile.

I won't pluck you from your patch.
I must face the truth.
You don't really know me.
You may know my name,
but you most definitely don't need me to grow.

My company is reserved
for all seasons and cozy dreams.
Occasionally coffee Sunday's,
if not, a lazy day be.
A week of fun, a week of smiles,
A week of food and everything in between.
I'm just glad,
it will all be guided,
by everything that is you and only you.
Will you join me on this year's seasonal dream?

-J. William-
Meet me under the same moon

Beautiful woman
wearing such poetic lotion.
Carrying a very strong and gentle
oceanic emotion.
Unraveling your rose corolla
upon our moon's light.
Not caring for the winds
and their whispers ready to fight,
Always prepared to throw a fist, but
also waiting in silent for someone's
loving and patient kiss.

-J. William-
Meet me under the same moon

You shine such a beautiful
and simple smile,
so bright and so warm,
that such brilliancy
latches on to my soul,
and for that split second,
my whole everything
warps into one single simper
between two very beautiful
and alluring dimples.

-J. William-
Meet me under the same moon

You my darling.
    You are the most
    beautiful,
    most intelligent,
    most kind, and the most
    compassionate
    soul, known to mankind.
    Strong, yet respectful
    to yourself and to others.
It was a very humbling
pleasure to have met
such a kindred soul such as
    yours.

Would you ever give me
the miraculous opportunity
to meet the hello that comes
from the voice of your heart.

-J. William-
Meet me under the same moon

51

Even though you are
slowly moving away from me.
I will hold on to you
  like the earth holds
unto its moon 🌙.
Desperately
 watching your
  unforgettable
gravitational pull
        move away
  from my life
    affecting my
whole entire world.

I love the way
your eyes,
your smile,
your soul, talk to me.
Speaking every word,
you dare not say.
Speaking in a language that
is very beautiful and very poetic.
Silent is the only way
that I could describe it, but slowly
I'm starting to dislike the fact that
your silence seems to know my name very well.

-J. William-
Meet me under the same moon

53

I just love seeing
your artsy and poetic pictures.
Especially the ones where
you show your beautiful smile.
They became poems without words
for my soul
to read and to imagine
all the wonders
behind all your beautiful
poetry.

Inside my heart lies a
beautiful butterfly.
Waiting for you to call him by name.
Waiting for The Her, within you
to ignite the spark between US.
Waiting for both butterflies to finally
meet in person for the very first time.
Just so that I can fall in love with all
your raw and naked insecurities.
All your beautiful, honest, and true emotions.
To witness that beautiful smile of yours.
Hopefully, maybe one day both our butterflies
can take flight into a never ending and timeless adventure,
across every sunrise and every sunset,
across every planet, and every galaxy,
and every universe with no end in sight
to this infinite love we both would share.

On one sunny day,
I saw something so spectacular
that it let my soul
so, tongue tied and at a loss for words.
I've been captivated by
something so beautiful,
something so pure,
something so true,
something I haven't witness in a very long time,
and now I long again to witness
those beautiful, gorgeous, and
powerful brown eyes again.

-J. William-
Meet me under the same moon

I would never in my whole entire life
change the way you are,
or would I ever try to criticize
the way you do things.
I might not know exactly what
you have been through, but
when I look into your eyes
they tell me that your
heart and your soul have been
beaten, broken, used, and
permanently scarred by situations
that absolutely nobody knows about,
except for you.
Now your heart and your soul over time
has grown to be so supple
yet so strong and
it's a beautiful thing to watch.
Why would I ever try to change or fix
anything about that;
and now that I know
that your heart is filled with love
and happiness, and humility, and strength,
and compassion waiting
to be set free.
I just hope I'm there to catch it
whenever you decide you are ready
to let it all loose.

Poetry is absolutely everywhere
In the world.
The air is filled with its
ghostly Spirits.
The ground shakes and balances its nature.
While the ocean dances to the verses
of its truthful music
and It's amazing how I can even
feel and sense poetry radiating
from your beautiful smile in the same manner.

-

-J. William-
Meet me under the same moon

I don't know
If it's you
or the moon
who keeps pulling me in,

but I'm confused,

I don't know
if to love or to dislike
the way
you and the moon
cast away the entirety
ocean of my soul
every time I go up to kiss
your beautiful shoreline.

And the lost child who marched into the stars.
Watching many fall into the hands
of their better halves.
From which one falls each night.
Leaving him wishing on falling stars.
A dream of crossing ranges of heavenly roses,
worn by one beautiful Angel,
just to tell her that
She is enough,
She is beautiful,
She is strong, and that,
He is not afraid of Her thorns.

-J. William-
meet me under the same moon

As we lay under a darkened sky,
filled with many bright and beautiful stars.
Your eyes are everything I see,
so magical, so captivating of my attention and
It's beautiful how each eye holds a different universe.
Containing beautiful black holes whose only purpose
is to capture men's hearts and soul.
The funny thing is that, ever since
the first time I laid eyes on you,
my everything was taken,
and I really don't want none of it back,
I wish for my heart
and my soul to remain in the abyss of your
beautifully darkened prison, knowing
I'll probably be serving
a life sentence of eternity.

You're beautiful,
you have acknowledged your light.
You convinced your shadow
you are someone worth following,
and there is no denying it
you no longer mask, but bask
on your own self worth
and unconditional love.
You have fallen in love with yourself
and finally began living
for and from yourself.
Living for and from your heart.
Living for and from
all truth, courage, and
empathetic compassion
your soul emits upon
anyone you touch eyes with.

I would rather gift you
a hundred flower crowns
made out of roses,
than a hundred diamonds
around your neck,
because that's just
the type of person you are.

Your beautiful soul is the
foundation to my creativity.
You literally became the reason why I write.
Seeing your gorgeous eyes
and your beautiful smile is like
a vacation for my soul.
One where I'm at peace on a beach,
staring out into the sunset
watching the sun melt into oranges and blues,
all while feeling you deep within my chest.
Such a freeing feeling to let it all out
onto the world for others to read.

With all the time in the world.
It would be nice to sit under the
same moon, the same stars, the same sun.
Watching the speeding bullet that is our lives,
slowing down to a mere crawl.
Bounded by no obligations.
To speak about endless love without
fear of the consequences.
To hear you talk for hours about
how much you love yourself and everything
in your world without end.
How beautiful would that be,
to sit next to you under the same sky.

-J. William-
Meet me under the same moon

*Anybody's writing, including mine
could never compare to the intense poems
that you alone could write with your eyes.
Easily burning through the thickest of paper.
Something so pure, so true, so deep.
Everything demanding to be felt without
a word ever being said.*

I am forever grateful, for your existence,
for I never saw you as the mesmerizing sunset.
I always knew you were the infinite light,
the infinite Sun.

The only therapy my soul
needs right now
is the sound of your voice.
To some, that voice may be an
array of meaningless words,
but for me they are
beautiful, poetic, and powerful messes
of inspiring elements of speech
put together to help cope
with my existence,
and now I'm craving nothing else but
to hear your healing voice
resonate into my soul once again.

-J. William-
Meet me under the same moon

I wish to be with you, by your side
and I will say it over and over.
I'll repeat it as many times as there are stars
in the heavens. Even if, for now,
they still remain silent and beautiful.

-J. William-
Meet me under the same moon

Fresh air in my lungs.
Friends in my heart.
Family in my soul.
And hopefully
Coffee with you one day.
What more could I ask for.
What more could I hope for.

-J. William-
Meet me under the same moon

She loved the way
how she found joy
in-between the sadness
of the rain.

How beautiful it is
to have something in common.

Ever since he left,
She locked up her heart and soul
with an encrypted
facial recognition passcode
that only he could unlock.
Leaving me and or the rest of everybody,
on an unknown journey.
To hunt and to scavenge,
in hopes,
that we stumble across a hack,
that leads directly
to her forbidden and hidden treasure
called love.

-J. William-
Meet me under the same moon

We sit at different spots
in silence in this world
wondering at the fact
that there will be another lifetime.
Vaguely knowing
that we are and have been already connected
and are actually sitting together
at a vibe-ing concert
in the heavens
under some, if not all stars,
and as you do your thing
and I do mine.
The question should be,
do we really want to wait
for another lifetime?
To sit together
in the same spot,
on this same world,
under the same stars.

I hope you manage to read this
because I want you to know,
You are beautiful,
You are strong, and very, very humble.
Your beautiful heart,
It has gone through so much pain,
so much sorrow and tears, so much hurt and loss.
You truly have been tested with
great tribulations, but still till this day
your heart and your soul continue to battle on,
with a smile on your face.
Wiping away those tears,
you secretly hide your pain from everybody else
who has no idea what you are going through.
Leaving you, wondering
"when will it all, ever just stop,
 when will it all, be just normal."
But please if you do manage to read this...
I just want you to know that
You are beautiful
And that you are, one of the strongest woman
I have ever had the pleasure of sharing a smile with
and please, if you ever need any kind of help, I'll be
more than happy to do whatever.

-J. William-
Meet me under the same moon

75

They say
kiss her mind,
and her body will follow.
I wonder
what would happen
if I were to
kiss her soul.
What would follow then?

-J. William-
Meet me under the same moon

It's a wonderful and strange thing
that a feeling can make you so confused.
A feeling that could make you feel
or pretend not to be true.
A feeling already caused
by two connected souls.
You can't hide something
that you already know is faith.
A feeling you want and need,
but for some reason
you desperately want to avoid.

-J. William-
Meet me under the same moon

You speak thru me
without a word ever being said,
just like the wind
who speaks and whispers
into the corolla of every rose flower.
Making them dance
in such a beautiful and confusing manner.

-J. William-
Meet me under the same moon

We can only take
with us memories and experiences
that are carved into
the mind and the heart of our soul.

-J. William-
Meet me under the same moon

Sun, Sunflower, Moon, Rose.
All within, above the earth.
She's in the sky, light so never ending.
I'm on the ground, dying and wishing,
Yet all our meetings and fate are but one.
Faith that we all go round
convincing our souls, we are meant for each other.
Everything us,
Strong, Gentle, and Eternal.

-J. William-
Meet me under the same moon

81

There are so many things
I love about you,
and one of them is knowing
how your body, mind, and soul
are in a place
where peace and love
are your priority.
And negativity has long been extinct
from your conscience.

-J. William-
Meet me under the same moon

Would you ever give my soul
the pleasure of taking his hand
with complete trust and
go on a universal, loving,
and beautiful adventure
to the moon and back?

I love, how She loves
walking around
with a happy heart,
a grateful Soul, with peace in mind,
and a very humbling and loving
smile to show,
and as time goes on
and She grows even stronger
with love and strength,
and beauty within that is perfect.
All I can hope for is that one day
She could share all that is Her,
with Me and My silent Soul.

-J. William-
Meet me under the same moon

From your eyes
stars fall like raindrops,
meteors striking my heart.
Wishing for a
never ending shower.

Her eyes a mystery puzzle
solved by no one.
Her smile a dictionary
of sadness and heartache.
Her soul a poetry book
for the hopeless and the romantic.
All too beautiful.
All too rare.
All too gorgeous not to read.
A long novel she is indeed,
that in seconds you will fall in love
but shall take you an eternity to forget her.

*Love,
such a beautiful
language
spoken by everyone
but only
understood by
the heart.*

-J. William-
Meet me under the same moon

87

Beautiful you,
be like the ocean my darling.
Beautiful, mysterious,
wild, and free.
I mean...
Why wouldn't the ocean want to be you?

-J. William-
Meet me under the same moon

I would, in a heartbeat surround myself
with the eternal flame within your heart.

Now, watch my soul burn for you
and only you.

-J. William-
Meet me under the same moon

*You are enough
and always will be.
You are beautiful.
You are strong.
You are kind.
You are gentle.
You are a beautiful rose flower.
So please,
don't look to change that, instead
look to love and share
all of you in even more variety.*

-J. William-
Meet me under the same moon

With her innocent heart
and her mind at peace.
She poses in beauty;
like a rose under a moonlit sky
and with a smile that is bright
and dark brown tints that glow.
Where memories softly
brighten her face,
and where thoughts
are serenely expressed.
Even the heavens dare not deny,
the magic that is met
within her eyes.

If you leave her alone,
She will begin to dance and sing
like a crazy person.
Under a light that belongs to her,
And I swear to you,
just one glance
and you, like the rest of the world,
will, fall in love.

In the visions of the night,
while gentle sleep veils my sight.
You come to me in dreams,
with a kiss and with words,
That only my heart and soul
could touch and hold.
Such a beautiful bliss
you are to me and my spirit.

-J. William-
Meet me under the same moon

I don't want to label this thing
you constantly share with my soul.
I don't want to label something
I really don't know what it is,
but I believe it, and I really want to practice
this infinite phenomenon with you.
Which is something bigger and more
beautiful than language,
something bigger than us.
Please if you know tell me.
How do you label, describe something
that only your soul and mine know about?
How do you describe this silent love between us?

-J. William-
Meet me under the same moon

I wonder,
was the moment we met,
where we shared a hello.
The one thing
the universe gave to me.
I'm scared to think or admit,
regretfully
that I completely
let it all go away.

-J. William-
Meet me under the same moon

The worlds noise has been
very quiet for me lately.
Sitting enjoying a warm cup of coffee.
Every sip tasting
like life,
like love,
like eternity,
like you.
…

…
God I never knew that
the moon,
the stars,
the sun,
the earth,
the galaxies,
the you and
that the universe would taste so good.
Everything so peaceful, so quiet,
so beautiful, so poetic.

-J. william-
meet me under the same moQn

below any star, any sun, or any moon,
or any sunny or Cloudy sky.
i seem to always find you.
Absolutely Everything about you
is always Everywhere around me.
i find you with me In everything
i do,
i see,
i feel,
i think,
i dream,
and Now, in absolutely every word
i seem to write.
you might see
a bunch of Letters, sentences, poems,
maybe nothing at all, but for me
there is a "U" in every single one of everything.

-J. William-
Meet me under the same moon

Being able
to look at myself
inside your beautiful eyes
and being able
to share your gorgeous smile
with the world,
is plenty enough
for me.

There is this one light
who I'm very fond of which,
immense.
The shadows of the most gorgeous girl
with a very beautiful smile is outlined.

I may have said that I don't know
where my inspiration comes from,
and if we, for some reason ever drift apart
like Moon and Sun.

I want to let you know that you
were, are, and will be forever
an inspiration, a muse
for the beating heart of my soul,
for many eternities to come.

And I'm very grateful that a strong
and kind light like you, found its way into my darkness.

-J. William-
Meet me under the same moon

99

Her light glows
and illuminates,
stimulating
everybody's sense
of sight.

Now I know why
I'm so blindly in love
with her lovely spirit.

-J. William-
Meet me under the same moon

A beautiful desire of mine
is to meet the soul within you.
The soul you purposely decide to hide away
from many who try to get close
to your beautiful self.
I'm not asking for much,
but I just want to know,
what is it that you hide beneath
all those flowers crowns and makeup.
I want to find out, what lurks beneath all that
air that you breath, whose sole purpose
is to haunt yours.
I just want to see it all,
all the raw cuteness that is beneath all
that is artificial.
I want to see all the canyons that were carved out
by all the tears you have cried over the years and
all the real genuine smiles with laughter
that you only show to yourself in the mirror.
I guess I am asking for much,
but that is the person, the soul
I desire the most to meet in person.

-J. William-
Meet me under the same moon

*A love like yours
is very hard to come by
in this universe,
almost non-existent
and irreplaceable.*

*Tell me,
Why do I keep contemplating
at the magical wonder
of talking to your beautiful soul?*

*Is it possible that
I'm scared
at the fact
that I think,
I actually found
a once in a lifetime
kind of love.*

I know exactly
how beautiful you are on the outside,
but that is not the reason
why I am so allured towards your persona.
There is something about you
I cannot figure out.
I guess it's the mystery within yourself
that you hide from everyone else
which keeps me so enticed in
finding out really how beautiful
you are on the inside.

Thank you for the light
that you are bringing to this world.
Please acknowledge yourself
for all the changes
that you have been willing to move through.
You have found your wings
and remembering how to soar.
Be brave, rekindle that fire
that has been flickering inside
that soul of yours,
and rise like a phoenix
just to show the world
how bright your light actually is.

-J. William-
Meet me under the same moon

Share yourself to the world
and to the universe.
Light up all that greatness you hide
beneath your beautiful and dark universe.

Undress yourself in world
that is hell bent on clothing you
in layers of false hope,
unwanted masks, and disillusioned truths.

Take it all off.
You will feel naked,
you will show your insecurities,
you will show your weakness,
but please never be scared to show your strength.

-J. William-
Meet me under the same moon

It took a lot of time,
hard work, and a lot of courage
but I finally fixed and rebuild
cupid's arrow,
and I'm thinking about
shooting for my moon once more,
let's hope it's not too late, and
that the beautiful target has not
yet been hit,
by someone else's
love arrow.

-J. William-
Meet me under the same moon

Stop with your absolute nonsense.
Even though you may not believe it.
You are absolutely
BEAUTIFUL
and I will continue to call you
BEAUTIFUL
absolutely every single day
for the rest of our eternity, until you
feel it all the way to the very core of your
BEAUTIFUL
soul.
Even when I'm not staring directly into your
BEAUTIFUL
eyes.

I'm just a lost soul
trying to find his purpose.
All while still
searching for his
beautiful her,
in this vast galaxy
of unknown nothing.

Even though I very strongly
dislike alcohol and liquor.
Every time I lay my eyes upon yours.
I act and feel drunk,
slur this, and slur that,
mumble this, and mumble that.
Unable to say what I actually want to say.
It has honestly become
drunken love.
A beautiful and drunken fact
that those eyes and that smile,
always leave me wanting more.
...
I guess I do like getting drunk.

-J. William-
Meet me under the same moon

She is the most beautiful
...
Her mesmerizing smile.
Her curious, caring, and loving heart.
Her affinity for at times running wild.
Her colorful mind.
Her strong, yet compassionate soul.
Her mysteries of the universe
hidden in her gorgeous and beautiful eyes.
She is indeed a very
beautiful phenomenon...
What a beautiful pleasure it is
to witness such a spectacle every now and then,
Thank you...

And into to my notebook I go,
with a pen in hand
and with an empty thought,
to lose my mind and
to find my soul.

-J. William-
Meet me under the same moon

You were a book
I was so eager
to read the plot,
but too scared
to even begin
reading the first page.

-J. William-
Meet me under the same moon

I keep her sweet words
and her beautiful smiles,
like old love letters locked away
inside my heart.
Every now and then
I open one,
just to stir up
the butterflies and reminisce
on the emotions and feelings
from that first day
where I had the opportunity to meet
such a beautiful and wonderful soul,
such as hers.

-J. William-
Meet me under the same moon

I never told you just how much you meant to me.
I never expressed the way you truly make me feel.
I never told you just how much warmth your light
brings to my soul.
I write it all the time, but never face to face
have I told you just how beautiful your eyes are
and how gorgeous your smile is.
I write it all the time, but never face to face
have I told you just how beautiful, strong, kind,
compassionate, loving, caring you are to yourself
and for others.
I'm sorry for not telling you that you were the one
I've been searching for. The one I talk to the moon about.
I'm sorry for never really inviting you to a nice coffee date
or something beautiful.
I'm sorry for passing up on the most beautiful experience
the universe has given me.
I'm sorry to write this, but I'm scared to think
that you have found love in someone else's arms,
but sometimes I do wish you would just
rip the band-aid off without warning.
It's okay let my soul cry. I will hold on to a belief
that your soul and my soul shared a passionate kiss
in a past lifetime
Under the Same Moon.

-J. William-
Meet me under the same moon

The night seals
her bottles filled with
stars and cries.
Tossing them into the ocean.
Watching them float onto the horizon.
Hoping they are to be lost forever
or to be found
by the lost boy who drowned
in search for love and light.

-J. William-
Meet me under the same moon

If consciousness really does
survive after death.
I will rest happy
for the rest
of my eternal life,
Knowing that
I still get to
have you on my thoughts.

-J. William-
Meet me under the same moon

Looking into
the person's eyes
of the one you love,
is the only way
two can fall in love
with both loving hearts.
It literally becomes
the only way someone
can actually
touch your heart.

-J William-
Meet me under the same moon

Stay smiling,
Stay loving,
Stay strong,
Stay soft and gentle,
because I'm
falling in love
with how
beautiful it looks
on you.

-J. William-
Meet me under the same moon

She was always so attracted
to a sunrise or a sunset kind of sky,
or a star filled with a shade of black kind of sky,
or any type of sky to be exact.
Like a force pulling on her towards the stars
as if she was one of them.

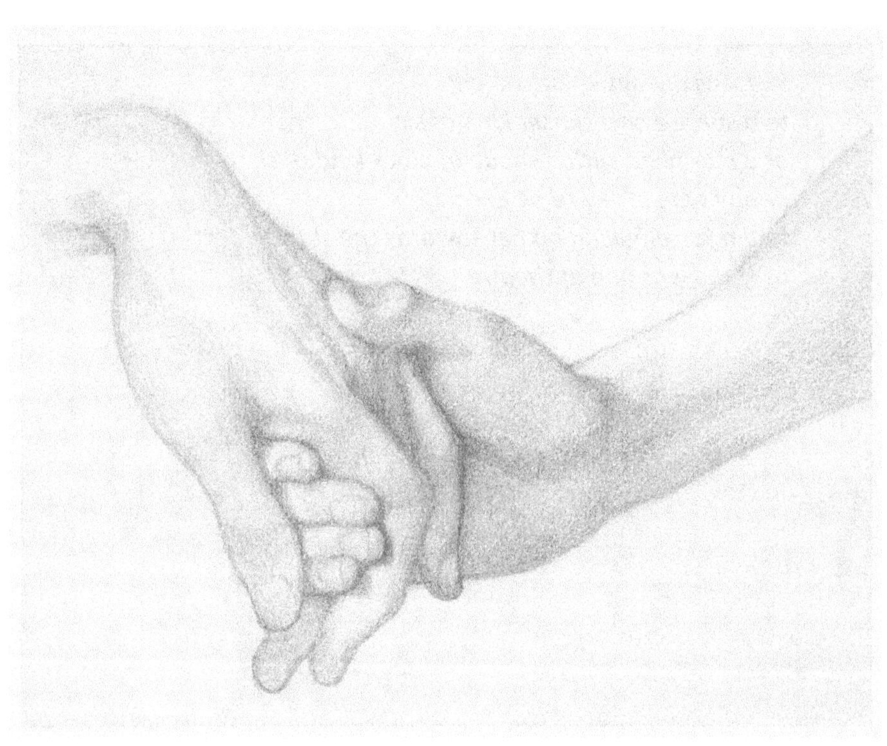

-J. William-
Meet me under the same moon

Once in my life
something astonishingly beautiful
startled me out of my normal routine.
At first, I thought it was a stunning sunrise
rolling towards me,
until I realized it was you
with the biggest and the most gorgeous smile
and the most beautiful eyes
in the whole entire world.
Even the universe could not compare
to the mystery and the light
that was shown that day.
.

Selfishly thinking it was all just for me.

-J. William-
Meet me under the same moon

Just once,
dig deep and deep dive
into your own consciousness.
Taking some time off
so that you may fall in love
with your own stars,
for you are full
of universal beauty
and wonder.

-J. William-
Meet me under the same moon

I bet you have heard
every single word in the dictionary
from men who wish
to grasp onto your heart.
That's why instead of words,
my proposal of attention is,
What instrument would you like me to
expertly strum with nothing but my heart,
to make waves of sweet poetic music,
hopefully making it to you,
touching both your heart and your soul,
just let me know when and where and
I'll be there with a list of songs
ready to carry in my feelings just for you,
and your opened heart.

-J. William-
Meet me under the same moon

A finale wish
a dying sun
will want you
to carry for
an entire lifetime.
Will always be,
their beautiful warmth,
memories, experience,
and specially forever
their wonderful love.
For it is now entrusted
upon you to share that same light
with the world.

-J. William-
Meet me under the same moon

*Words so soft like a gentle prayer,
swirling from her warm morning coffee.
Her eyes the color of
everything strong,
yet kind, gentle, and beautiful
peering over the rim of her cup.
If you were to look closer through the
steam of her sweet morning nectar
you shall and will catch a glimpse of
her raw and wonderful soul.*

-J. William-
Meet me under the same moon

Give me a chance
to share at the very least
a silent moment
with you
and your soul.
Let me experience
such a
true and honest moment
with your
beautiful presence.

-J. William-
Meet me under the same moon

Keep the comfort
of my soul and the happiness of my heart
locked away
inside your caring and loving heart,
for I would cherish that
more than a chest
filled with the finest of rubies
and shiniest of diamonds.

The sun is the poet.
The moon is the lover,
both dreaming
of sharing a beautiful moment
on the same horizon
where the stars are falling.

Her eyes
      very beautiful,
    so divine,
like rays of falling petals
     on the horizon.
Sharing with the world
     Her Light and Love,
    while screaming
    the pain She hides within.

-J. William-
Meet me under the same moon

*She's the kind of soul
        to hold back
      Her ocean,
just to let the life-giving Sun
time to soar and rest
on Her shouldering waves.*

Beautiful,

two rose vines filled with thorns
dripping tears of hatred,
> *sadness,*
> *and sorrow.   Tears of joy,*
> *happiness,*
> *and peace of mind*
and some of them, only some,
filled with a gentle, flexible will,
to fall in love with each other.

-J. William-
Meet me under the same moon

I could, in a heartbeat
spend my
entire life savings
in order to buy,
but seconds of your time
to be spent on me.
Even if all I get
is but smile in return.

-J. William-
Meet me under the same moon

Alas for the worn
and the tired soul,
whether in youth or in age
has experienced life changing tragedies
that no one but themselves
could understand,
and over time
their life has grown and developed
and will continue so,
but still no soul
is more profoundly sad
than them who
beautifully and poetically
smile and laugh too much.

-J. William-
Meet me under the same moon

A poem is private
and very interior.
Thoughts and feelings
that are very personal to oneself.
Writing down the deepest
of conversations between
soul, heart, and mind
and I choose to show
the world my poetry.
Poetry that defines the
connection between your soul and mine.
Poetry that defines the
connection between us and the universe,
just like our sun and moon.
Poetry that defines the
connection between me and my world.

-J. William-
Meet me under the same moon

I fell in love
with your smile
but even more in love
with the unexpected laughter
you not only share with me
but with everybody
you care for.
A rare gift indeed my soul
could not steal,
For I am way too much in love
with how you open up the lips of your heart,
just to show the pearls
that radiate from your soul.

They say flowers
are nature's jewels.
A symbol of love's truest language
to express many rich sentiments
that are able to replace any word or sentence
that you, myself, or anyone else
may be too shy to utter.
I have sent you my offering
of those colorful nature jewels,
something small,
but with a big loving intention
to make that goddess within yourself smile,
a smile so bright and so warm.
In hopes that you bless me of being worthy
of receiving that smile towards my direction,
and in lighting up a darkened man.

It is a beautiful feeling
that you are on this same world as me.
Staring, talking, and wishing
under and upon
the same moon and stars.
Mesmerizing and appreciating
the same morning sky and sun.
A beautiful feeling indeed
that you belong
to the same universe as I.
I wonder,
I know of your present soul
in this infinite world,
do you know of mine?

-J. William-
Meet me under the same moon

Just like you,
there is no trifling with nature
and it's infinite power.

Just like you,
nature is beautiful, true, pure,
unbelievable, and breathtaking.

Just like you,
nature is also strong, fierce, powerful,
and very untamable.

Nature is you and you are nature.
No wonder I can't grab a hold
of your chaotic beauty.

We are
but a moment
in time.
Nothing less,
nothing more
but what I love
the most is knowing
that you and I
are eternals in a
forever space
in between
the word
  -L O V E.

-J. William-
Meet me under the same moon

You are one in seven billion.
One fingerprint
in this vast ocean
of life, oh so
very impossible to find,
but lucky me I found you,
perfect just how I imagined you.
Now how do I bait you into my life
so that I can catch that
wild heart of yours.

The simple man within me,
just wants to thank you
for the beautiful miracle
of giving me the chance and the privilege
to have met someone like you,
and to get to know
your beautiful name,
your beautiful energy,
but more importantly
your beautiful smile.

-J. William-
Meet me under the same moon

Your heart,
Your mind, and
Your soul
became my whole life.
You see,
Life is like a gorgeous flower
where love
is the honey of it all.

-J. William-
Meet me under the same moon

Do you feel it?
This very intimate connection
that you and I have created, all
through two smiling souls.

We know absolutely nothing
about each other's life, but still
this connection we share makes it
seem like we have known each other
for an eternity,

even though
all I really know is just your name,
I am thankful and consider myself
the luckiest man in the
whole entire universe to of had
shared a once in a lifetime
smile to smile connection with you.

What a beautiful miracle it was indeed
knowing such a presence as yours.

-J. William-
Meet me under the same moon

The sun so shy and mighty
speaks so highly in eloquence
to an audience of stars,
of the moon who is a bright and beautiful force
filled with so much universal love.
He goes on and on about wanting nothing
but to be closer to the moon
and to shine a never-ending light
to brighten any darkness or sadness
that the moon may hold,
So, the sun sends countless messages
towards the moon through shooting stars,
in hopes that they are being listened to and read.
Always wishful thinking that maybe
one day the moon will send back
a huge galactic sign saying
"let's break the silence between each other,
I shall be your moon,
but only if you become my one and only sun".

-J. William-
Meet me under the same moon

My spirit gazes
up into the sky.
Wishing, reading,
and falling in love
with the infinite stars,
that are the poetry
of heaven.

Life no longer
chance or fate.
Unsought before
my door I see.
On wings of fire
and steads of steam.
The world's great wonders
of your love come to me.
Far more than all
I ever dared
to dream.

-J. William-
Meet me under the same moon

You truly are
mysterious
in its most
simplistic definition
of the word,
and I think
that is the reason
why my soul
is so crazy attracted
to you.
I just can't seem
to figure you out.

-J. William-
Meet me under the same moon

The truth guys,
I'm dying.
The reason, Mortality.
It might be sooner, or it might not,
I don't really know, so in the meantime
I shall enjoy this moment, right now.
Not spent in a rocking chair
with a seatbelt on,
but out doing anything and everything
that my heart desires
Even if it is not how I plan it to be.
Love, gratitude, compassion, and humility
is all I need as passengers
in my vehicle of thoughts and actions
to fulfill my soul's desire.

-J. William-
Meet me under the same moon

The presence of the sun
could be felt when standing next to her.
The presence of the moon
could be felt when holding her hand.
The presence of a galaxy
could be felt when a kiss is respectably
place on her forehead,
and her lips, her lips were something different.
A whole entire and unexplainable universe
could be felt, with a kiss to her beautiful lips.

Since the first moment
our souls met each other.
There is never a moon
that doesn't pass by,
nor never a sun
that always rises.
Where you aren't
on the thoughts
of my soul's mind.

He would do anything
for a chance
to grow a pair of wings.
Desperately longing
to touch the sky
and to fly high unto
the moon,
just for a kiss
from this beautiful
source of light,
he is so crazy
attracted to.

-J. William-
Meet me under the same moon

On earth
consciousness guides your being,
and in the heavens
you are being watched
as destiny, strength, and virtues
are written upon your forehead.
So, never let
ego, hatred, or anger
within your beautiful thoughts
or of others create phantoms
you invoke to silence one
and to dethrone the other,
for acts of this life,
will carry on to the next.

*Let me spoil you
with whatever it is
that you may desire.*

*Just so that I may
get the chance to stare
deeply into your eyes
without interruptions,*

*just to lose myself
and to see the magic
of the stars
glisten within them.*

Third attempt at love in turning dreams into reality.
Where a hello has not yet seen a lifetime.
Is it you, is it me,
is it your reality who is not ready or is it mine?
I guess it doesn't matter.
I shall forever continue to dream for you, the perfect roses,
as many roses as there are diamonds in the water of the sea,
for you respectfully deserve every single one. And as many
as there are dreams in this childish head, for I owe it
to my soul to give you as many as I can.

Shakespeare once said that,
"A good heart is worth gold".

Well yours my darling
it is worth more than just gold.
It's a very rare, one of a kind,
and irreplaceable jewel.
Very precious and very beautiful
with all its pointed and curved edges.
I can't even begin to imagine
how much your soul is worth
and in finding out,
how a man like me,
can purchase such a divine jewel.

-J. William-
Meet me under the same moon

Everyone's heart,
including mine,
must in a measure
be alone in this world,
but why is it,
that my heart
has reasons that not even
my soul
could understand.

We have control
of so much, but nothing
is less in our power
than the heart.

We are far from
commanding the poor
fragile thing.

We are forced
to obey and to feel
all of its complexions
and confusions.

Affecting not just
our lives, but
our whole entire world.

-J. William-
Meet me under the same moon

I sit my days away
at a shoreline
that belongs to the universe.
My soul quietly singing along,
luring a dream
of being in the arms
of her waves,
just so that she can carry me
far far away.

-J. William-
Meet me under the same moon

Standing by the beach
in the middle of the night
is where I want to be.
Staring at your light
reflected onto the ocean.
Me surrounded by darkness.
Thinking should I jump into
your infinite waters of love.
Knowing that such power is infinite
in creating strong and mesmerizing waves.
Which in fact, can and will
drown my own heart and soul
into your chaotic ocean.
Never to be released again.

"Well I hope not".

The fruit of your soul
un-wrinkles itself
upon the
brightest and strongest
of stars.

"I fell in love".

That is the only
expression
I can think of,
and still I remain
at the mercy of your light.

-J. William-
Meet me under the same moon

If I was given one wish.
My wish would be,
to spend infinite amounts
of precious moments by your side,
and if for some reason
it never happens in this lifetime,
which in fact we know will have to end.
Maybe one day we could be together
in a forever when we leave our bodies
and become our own stars,
to fall in love and wonder around
all over this vast universe of ours.

-J. William-
Meet me under the same moon

You have no idea and possibly
might not even care,
but every time I see your smile
it drives me crazy.
It's like every night
looking at the moon.
Wanting and craving
to talk,
to touch,
to hold
the very core of your light,
but still knowing that every night,
it moves slowly away
from the tips of my fingers.
Regretting every centimeter
that you move away
and me not finding the courage
to do anything about it.

-J. William-
Meet me under the same moon

I use sun and moon
in a lot of my writing because
they resemble so much of
you and I.
Both so connected but
still remain so

distant

I guess one good thing
is that once we vanish
immortality awaits us all
at the end of life.
Hopefully in that universe,
there is a moon that is willing
to be crazy enough
to at the very most
be close enough to such a
lonely and blazing atmosphere.

-J. William-
Meet me under the same moon

We suffer
because we desire,
give up desire, and
we end our suffering,
but the real question is,
how does one
desire to give up
the one thing we desire
the most.
I guess that's my point
I'm always trying
to figure out myself.

When a soul finds his mate.
One minute of love from
his greatest pleasure of life
can become his very existence,
the whole,
the very life breath of his heart.
What a beautiful necessity of
our nature to love,
and I'm eternally grateful
that I got to share
a special one-minute connection
with you and your beautiful soul.

-J. William-
Meet me under the same moon

You, beautiful blue moon
are you scared to fall in love,
because I sure am.
You are constantly surrounded
by stars who wish to take your light.
I just want to be among
the chosen few who are closest.
Not to steal, but to give my light instead,
for whenever you begin to shadow
your infinite self.

-J. William-
Meet me under the same moon

I wish to have
a conversation
with your soul.
A nice and simple
coffee date
on a Sunday morning.
Where I wish
to talk about
every common emotion
and feeling you feel
in the most uncommon way,
just to make you
feel extra special,
extra beautiful.

A brilliant universe within her soul,
an all giving loveliness.
Her sacred starry shade of dim,
everything light and dark,
different and very beautiful.
Composed of countless suns, and worlds,
and moons, and stars that are
full of light, and life, and motion.
A different and beautiful
language she is to be read and learned,
and I wouldn't mind
talking Her fluently.
Even if it does end up taking me
an entire lifetime.

-J. William-
Meet me under the same moon

The essence of your being is
what I'm mostly madly in love with,
to me, you became
the golden star at night
that lights up
an entire ocean
making ripples of waves crash
into the heart of one's earthly ground.

-J. William-
Meet me under the same moon

Pictures and poetry
are loopholes of escape
for the soul.

They are considered
consolers of loneliness
and a great relief to the jaded mind.

Windows to imprisoned thoughts.
Windows that only you
my beautiful muse
can open and unlock.

With nothing but
a picture and a smile.

Passions are the winds
that fill
the sail of a vessel.

"Set sail for her
        heart I go".

but the only way to reach
such a divine and
beautiful paradise
is to use her,
and only her glorious and
never ending winds.

-J. William-
Meet me under the same moon

It's beautiful
how every moment
of every night
and every moment
of every day,
*   in between.*
There is a never ending
dream of your moon,
next to my sun.
Two lights, day and night.
Under and above
the same time.

-J. William-
Meet me under the same moon

If I were to die tomorrow
it will be ok, because
I lived happy,
I loved happy,
and I have enjoyed
the happiness from the souls
who I care for,
and I'm eternally grateful for
the rest of my eternal life,
that I get to keep these treasures
locked away deep within
the heart of my soul.

They say a universe
hides within
the heart of our souls,
and sometimes I wonder,
does your beautiful heart
contain a galaxy just for me
or was I just made into a
deteriorating meteorite
to be watched and gazed,
passing by slowly,
vaporizing never to be seen again.

-J. William-
Meet me under the same moon

How do you say
the simplest of things
to the one you love.

Who's boldness,
and toughness,
and independence
flow through her
gorgeously and gracefully.

Who's honesty,
personal and public respect,
and compassionate heart
make her the most perfectly beautiful
human being in this world.

Who's mind, body, and soul
shine brighter than any daylight
given by the sun or any moonlight
shown by the moon.

How does one win over such a beautiful
and one of a kind,
universal heart like hers.

-J. William-
Meet me under the same moon

Sitting back listening
to the heavy but silent winds
from your soul.
Passionately kissing,
shattering and molding at the same time,
such a fragile part of my heart,
reminding me
what it feels to actually
fall in love once again.

I want your soul
  to kiss
    my heart,
just so that I can
  see and feel
    what actual fire
  will feel like
inside my chest.

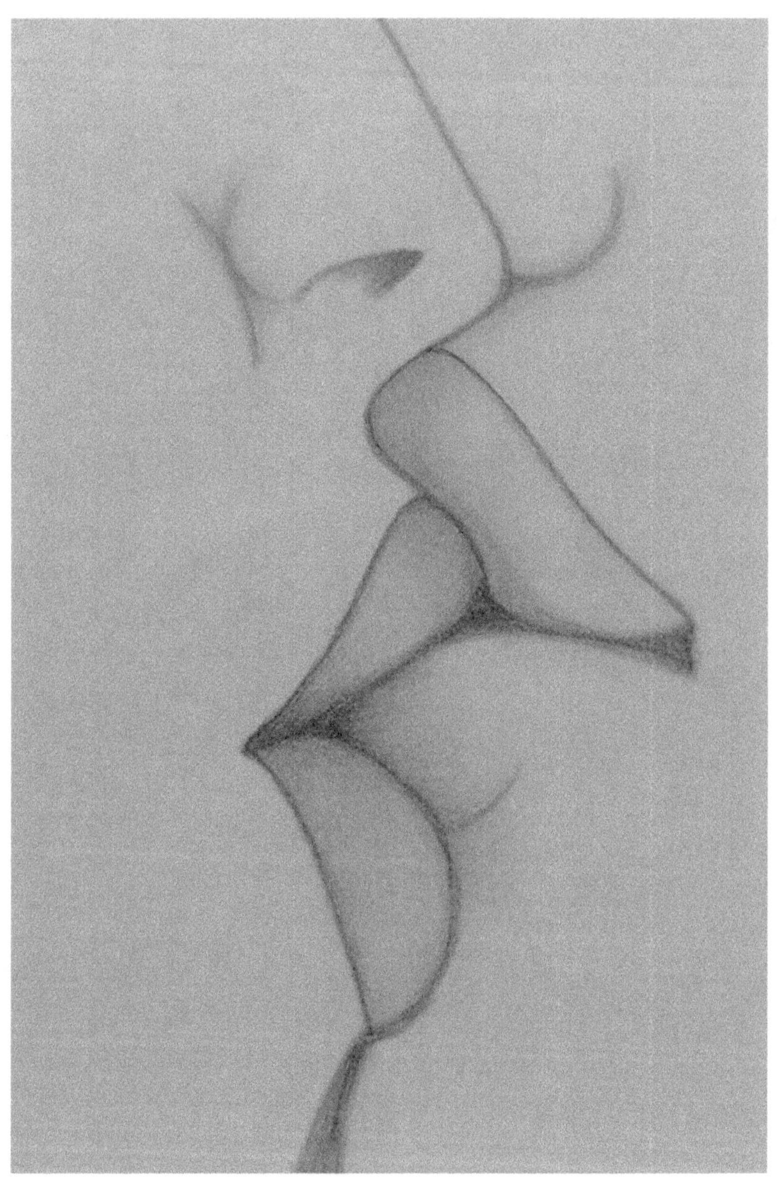

Deep within the heart
that your soul carries.
In a bed of everything wonderful
lay soft, gentle
and beautiful
spoken words.

Poetry,
that can only
be read, felt and or
released by a
kindred and
lucky soul.

There are ways
in which to become undone,
for example;

stare into my eyes
and unravel
all what you are.
Let the tears
that run over your smile
show, what the words
that you speak
cannot define.

He found Her,
just when She thought no one
would see Her.
He opened the door to witness
that only desire followed.
He welcomed Her soul,
Her flaws,
Her sadness,
Her love,
all She wanted was to be loved.
All She wanted was to feel needed.
Lucky and beautiful it was,
when He found Her, but
has She found Him yet.
Has She noticed that there is someone
right there wanting and waiting
to catch Her as She falls.
Waiting to finally get noticed and
to actually have a real genuine
and long conversation with Him,
about Her and only Her.

*Let me be your sea
to act as a mirror,
so that you can stare
at your reflections.
Wondering and praising
your own existence,
your own light,
your own beautiful curves,
because without you
I am nothing but
still water.*

-J. William-
Meet me under the same moon

In a sea of grass,
undaunted by stems
long enough to cocoon
the wild flower that you are.
Standing strong and tall
like a sunflower
under a blue line sky,
which covers the pulse
of your vitality,
making yourself stronger
every single day.
You truly are,
a beautiful power and magical love
who learned to conquer
this wonderful world of ours.

-J. William-
Meet me under the same moon

Our souls they are constantly searching
for their one and only true love,
sometimes waiting 500 years or more.
Well it must be true, because
that is my only explanation for the way
I felt when my soul finally met yours.
500 years' worth of love and emotions
that have built a connection so strong
with such an incredible bond.
Defining the unexplainable rush of divine peace
and calm I get when you are near.
The fluttering of my heart with
the warmth of your touch.
The bliss of your laughter and
the depth of your eyes
kissing the heart of my soul.
Feelings that were once trapped, now released
into the air that you breath.
Every single thing gorgeous and beautiful
about you, made perfectly for me.

-J. William-
Meet me under the same moon

You and I know exactly
how it feels to die young,
knowing that the only thing
holding together the pieces
of our hearts,
melted away the day we
lost our hope.
Feeling the cracks grow
deeper and longer,
knowing that the only thing
that would ever put them back together.
Would be the sound of
their voice,
their warmth,
their gentle, humbling,
nurturing hands,
their beautiful love.
.

I just wish I had the chance to say
goodbye and that I love you,
to your beautiful soul, but please
forgive me, I am truly, truly sorry
for not being there when you
needed me.

As I lay, wide awake
on a different day,
full of thoughts, full of words.
Ink stains upon the bed I lay.
Blood mingles within them.

"Is he dead" a voice begins to sing.
Next to him lies a pen
like a broken wing.
His hands clutched poems,
as he hugs them next to his heart.

Why is it that the easiest things
that we feel, seem the hardest things to say.
He found the courage and
was brave enough to say
but one stated piece.

Never in a million years did he believe
that she would ever do this to him.
And as he lay's in bed, wide awake
wondering, how did a poet like her
managed to kill him with words
that she hasn't even spoken yet.

This invisible karmic thread of string,
which ties soulmates together.
A thread the colour of red
as in passion, as in love.
A thread, a knot, a bond
that can never wither
or truly separate something
that is believed to be genuinely unbreakable;
and no matter where they are
or how far away they are from each other,
they could be in a different dimension.
They will always find one another.
This is destiny, this is love, and
what a wonderful feeling it is knowing that
the universe granted every soul
a reflection, a mirror of themselves, a kindred spirit.
A person who brings you
to your own existence, your own attention.
A person who shows you everything
that is holding you back so that you can
change your life for the better,
because close together they are
as they were intended to be.

-A whole.

-J. William-
Meet me under the same moon

There is no doubt
that those souls
who bring the sun with them
through the door, always smiling.
Helping those in the dark
while pointing to the starry skies;
guarding, protecting, reassuring
everyone by their truthful and loving words.

Those souls who are sadly gone,
will always and forever be heartfully missed,
but every now and then
you run into beautiful angels who smile
so bright, believing for everyone
that someone's Sun is never truly gone.

-J. William-
Meet me under the same moon

The eternal flame you have within
so bright, so beautiful.
Which lit the spark within my soul.
Touching every part of my being,
and as I wear a broken torn piece
on my sleeve,
I just want you to know
that I can still feel
the soft burnt traces you left on
the horizon of my skin
from that moment when our souls
were in a fiery dance,
while exchanging in a never ending
hot and ragged breath of swirling steam.
You literally,
set my soul on fire.

-J. William-
Meet me under the same moon

We all have something
that dwells within our bodies.
A soul, unique and special,
like one snowflake in many billions,
but it seems that is has become
a norm where humans have learned
to give their hearts away.
While very few
know how to give their soul as a remedy
for true and honest and compassionate love.
A norm that it has become rare, weird and
uncommon to meet with a genuine soul,
for every thousand conversations,
It participates in one.
Why hide?
Let your soul roam freely for it is
everything that you are, true and pure.
Open yourself and listen to its silent whispers
calling your name, pleading to open
the lock from the sealed cage you keep it in.

-J. William-
Meet me under the same moon

Look into my eyes
and without a sound.
Let your soul express
what your lips cannot.
Show me the way
to understand everything
that is hidden behind
those beautiful dark brown
tinted windows
that lead directly to
the heart of your soul.

Tears are the showers
that rain and fertilize our earth,
add a little sunlight
to those tears from a smile
and we have created
a beautiful rainbow
for both our souls
to gaze upon.

One thing is for sure,
human love is not so worthless or forgetting
that you could sweep it under the rug.
It is giving, beautiful, eternal,
and it's within us all.
And my wish for you
and for everybody else
is that you become
the blossom of hope, courage, and strength
that will never wilt away.
To share it with yourself
and with everybody you are and will be loving.

I will forever and always say,
that your eyes and your smile
are filled with
emotions, truth, and empathy
that are far beyond the word,

perfect.

Three thousand
written novels will never show
the truth, the clarity, the blessed reward.
Than three uttered words
said from the heart of your soul.

*Thank you
  for sharing
such a true, honest,
  and beautiful moment
with me and my soul.
A memory I will
  carry with me
and cherish for an
  eternal lifetime.*

-J. William-
Meet me under the same moon

Your eyes filled
with so much
love and chaos.
Waiting to be set free
at any given moment.
I just hope
that I'm worthy enough
to be in
that present moment,
to witness, to dance, to comfort
the fireworks
of a million stars,
all which light up
your beautiful pair of brown eyes.

-J. William-
Meet me under the same moon

Take me back
to the days
when small moments
spent with you
were little,
but remained
infinite and limitless.

-J. William-
Meet me under the same moon

He who is intoxicated
with wine or liquor
will be sober again
throughout the course
of the night, but
he who is intoxicated
with your love
will never recover
his senses until his last breath.

A beautifully desired calamity
it is indeed.

-J. William-
Meet me under the same moon

You filled a great part within me
with something beautiful and
heavy
that I will carry and cherish
every day for the rest of my eternal life.

-J. William-
Meet me under the same moon

Her soul was too bright
for anybody to dim.
Her hope too loud
for anybody to shut down.
Her heart too big
for anybody to break,
and her passion for love and life
too strong
for anybody to handle.
Which made her
the strongest woman
on this planet.
Loved by so many,
including myself.

-J. William-
Meet me under the same moon

The sun alleviates
any shade of dark within the soul,
but the one time
you let me take a peek inside
all I saw were rainy clouds.
Which is good because
like the sun, rain
also washes and soothes all
that is sad and dark,
and you my darling
you have been through enough.
I say let the music of the rain
within your soul go on forever.
I'll be right there dancing
with you till the very end.

-J. William-
Meet me under the same moon

Our souls
they know
of a sentence
of words and poetry
not yet invented
by the human mind.
They truly know
how to describe
the universe
that connects
your moon and my sun.
Through a simple touch
and a simple stare
into each other's hearts.

Like the moon
which illuminates
the dark in a wonderful
and pleasant silence.
Your soul does
the same within
the world of my heart.

*I don't like
seeing you cry,
but seeing those tears
that run down your cheeks.
They show me,
that they are proof
of a never-ending love
you have for life, love, and
everyone in it.*

-J. William-
Meet me under the same moon

Love really has nothing to do
with wisdom, or experience, or logic.

It is but a simple breeze,
sweeping our souls of their feet,
while both you and I
watch and gaze
as our moonlit spirits
fly high unto the sky.

Dancing to the tune
of our hearts beating below.

-J. William-
Meet me under the same moon

My mind, my body, and my soul,
weigh heavier than usual
and I strongly believe
that you are the cause for it.
You secretly snuck
a little piece of you
in my everything.
Now it has become
a part of me
that I can't seem to shake off.

-J. William-
Meet me under the same moon

Your soul within its heart
carries the sea
of a million earths.
Very strong, very witty,
very nurturing to the touch.
Filled with such
enlightening vitality
making this the most
beautiful fact in my universe,
but also, the most mysterious.

*Thoughts are an
illusory thing
keeping you from
expansive freedom
your soul is destined to have,
so why do we let these
thoughts separate us
from our present moments
in this world.*

The voice
of your soul
sings a melodic duet with mine,
which someway, somehow
ends up filling my heart
with something
I have never felt before.
A melody so calming, so beautiful
making it hard for me
to understand the heaviness
of such a poetic emotion.

-J. William-
Meet me under the same moon

Walk with me by an ocean side
to watch the sunset melt
into oranges and blues,
just like my heart
which constantly melts for you.
Give me your hand,
so that I may pull you close
in between my arms,
because you and I will be
forever dancing under the stars.
This way I get the chance
to melt under and over
the entirety of your soul.

-J. William-
Meet me under the same moon

"For woman's love"
* -I mean self-love,*
is boundless,
just like the sea.

"Your love"
* -I mean my love,*
is full of passion,
just like the air that we breath.

"Your beautiful soul"
* -I mean my soul,*
is unique and one of a kind,
just like one rose petal amongst billions.

"You are beautiful"
* -I mean we're beautiful.*

In all honesty,
   I am but very simple.

      One star,

in search of a universe
who wants humility, compassion,
love, happiness, loyalty,
and adventure.

-J. William-
Meet me under the same moon

No cord or cable
can draw so forcibly
or blind, so fast,
as love can do,
with just
a single strand of passion.

Let's you and I
wrap ourselves
in such a rare
piece of simplicity.

The waterfalls from the sky
nourish our land and our living growth.
Creating streams of life,
where we bathe in its glory,
where we shelter from its harshness and
where we sweetened our lips with delight.
It's a beautiful fact
that your tears, like water.
I can feel and touch your love
in the same manner.

Meet me under the same moon

I'm a tired rose,
dried up and falling,
but I don't want you to lose your love just yet,
my beautiful rose.
We both are becoming
who we need to be in life,
and I know
I should be giving you
all my attention in watering
your roots, your thorns,
your beautiful petals
and I'm glad that I found
such a beautiful love,
from such a beautiful creature
on this crazy world of ours,
but this desperate feeling we both carry
inside our hearts, it's making it difficult
for both you and I to grow as one.
I guess we both are just waiting
for that perfect moment
where the sun, the moon, and the stars
hide behind some clouds for just
a second or two, and for us to watch and feel
the rain fall and wash our tired souls.

Underneath the stars,
hearing nothing
but the human noise
we sat their making.

Your heart,   my heart,
beating,   communicating.

Not one of us moving.
Themselves, ourselves
enjoying our beautiful presence.

-J. William-
Meet me under the same moon

It is as old as creation
and yet as young and fresh as ever.
A kiss to be planted upon
the lips of a lover.
Setting your soul free
from a moment of chaos.
Being able to hear
the rhythm of the water,
all while dancing with the waves,
in a universal sea of love.

It is the sad truth
when they say
our thoughts can betray us
and be fools,
for I am a fool
thinking that our souls
were possibly connected at heart.
Night and daydreaming
that I could one day hold you
in-between my arms.

-J. William-
Meet me under the same moon

All I want
is to fall in love
with the way
she rises from bed.

To cherish
all the in-betweens

and then to watch her fall
back against it again.

Her heart,
such a fragile vessel
learned to control
such merciless oceans.
She became one with the deep sea,
and for a moment
like a drop of rain,
she noticed my presence,
but only for just a moment,
until I started fading away
deep within her mysterious,
vastly, and forgotten depths.

-J. William-
Meet me under the same moon

How does one
stare out into an
infinite abyss
of absolutely nothing,
but pure blankness,
but still holding hope
that one day a beautiful moonlight
will light up the lilies into candles,
to breath small breaths of light
into a darkened and forgotten soul.

-J. William-
Meet me under the same moon

What a beautiful miracle
it was to meet
your beautiful moonlight,
filled with so much love,
such divine vitality
which produced
and restored life
to the dimming sun
of my soul.

-J. William-

Meet me under the same moon

And just like that,
the spark is ignited.
Two souls connected at heart.
Both eyes locked
into each other's divine self,
almost to a point of no return.
Me glancing and starring into
those mesmerizing eyes
is all what makes sense now.
Watering and loving all what you are
my beautiful rose flower,
is exactly what I was made for.

-J. William-
Meet me under the same moon

Look at those smiling eyes.

The chaotic sea storms
within her growing
beautiful and old.

Breaking the silence,

the heavens listened
while she sang
the truths of a
divine and lost love.

-J. William-
Meet me under the same moon

I am carrying loneliness,
I will not lie to you.
Sometimes feeling as though
my words didn't reach certain stars.
Believing that's what loneliness
is, was, will.

I guess I will remain waiting
for the impossible to happen.

Mesmerized by your light,
standing there
smiling,
looking out
into the stars,
watching the moon
caress, outlining your curves.
Making time stop for a second,
realizing how true love
can make you feel very infinite.

-J. William-
Meet me under the same moon

He credited her
with a number of virtues,
of the existence of her
bright and beautiful light,
but me,
like all others remain
simple shadows in a pursuit
of a beautiful blue
moonlight rose,
just to keep us alive.

It's raining
and it's that delicate time
to begin stitching the words
that have been spoken and
heard by billions.
Creating messages
to be taped
on every cloud passing by.
Hopefully making it to you,
So, you can watch every single
raindrop fall down
stitched with your name
on every single
one of them.

The world,
      real or imagined.
You and I
    exist.
We met for a reason.
Our souls,
they met
in a past lifetime.
Now,
they long to meet
once again.

-J. William-
Meet me under the same moon

Far in the distant
appearing beautiful and stunning
awaits, a gorgeous star
carrying forgotten truths.
Illuminating an unexplainable brilliance.
Waiting to explode
all her honesty
upon our universe.

You, so strong and beautiful,
just like the morning sky
pouring everywhere your golden glory,
touching everyone's soul,
including mine.

Everything that is high and
everything that is hidden
deep within the heart of my soul
is illuminated by the guidance
of your eyes, and
I wouldn't want it any other way.

-J. William-
Meet me under the same moon

Seeing the depths of your beautiful
and raw emotion,
like the deep blue and dark mesmerizing ocean.
Holding specks of stolen sunlight,
There the hearts of your admires lay drowning
with nothing but delight.

And then I realized...
I was perfectly, beautifully, and poetically
falling in love with everything true and pure.
It just took me a while to figure out
that your smile
was the only light I needed to see.

I want that no matter what happens
you get the best out of me,
you get my everything, heart and soul,
the world gets the rest,
Kind of love

241

Somewhere in a forever,
I'm still waiting
for your blessings
to line up with my stars.

-J. William-
Meet me under the same moon

242

Have I ever mentioned,
how beautiful it is
that your smile is able to
convey feelings of
courage, peace, and honesty
that a thousand words
could never do.

-J. William-
Meet me under the same moon

I was walking down this road
wanting to see the world,
while looking for a soul,
and I ran into you
with galaxies for eyes
eternity for a smile,
and beautiful wings for courage.

-J. William-
Meet me under the same moon

Summer nights
the storms are brewing.
One unique leaf in the winds
amongst the thousands.
You wonder is it going with the flow
or is it fighting the treacherous storm?
I guess it doesn't matter,
either way it remains
strong, gentle, and wild.
How could one not fall in love
with such universal power
in nature.

My heart and soul
over past conflicts of reality
have invigorated, cleansed, and have established
truths about me.
I am now brave, empathetic, wild, and giving.
And I'm always in a constant search for
beautiful art, knowledge, adventure, and love.

-J. William-
Meet me under the same moon

I'm constantly
writing to you, about you,
and a connection
my soul has with yours.
My heart thinks, it's beautiful,
but my thoughts
are consistently wondering
if you really are listening.

Are you listening?

You literally
stepped inside
the heart of my soul,
little by little
making it heavier
but full once more.

So chaotically beautiful it was,
to try and teach this love-sick soul of mine
to swim under the ocean of your heart,
when clearly, I was drowning.

Every brave soul
who found courage, hope, and love
never ceased its crusade to earn it.
It's important to remain
always laughing, always smiling,
always shining, and always loving.

-J. William-
Meet me under the same moon

Undressing my soul before the sunset.
Watching the stars beginning to glisten.
Reminiscing before all thoughts.
Remaining motionless,
desiring to find myself in the sea.
Contemplating that one point amid the infinite.
Realizing that in all reality
It's just the sea and me.
Hoping that is becomes the beginning of everything,
and if nothing ever changes,
I shall remain still, to be different
among what is hard to comprehend.

251

*I will be forever convincing myself
that us mesmerizing and wishing
under the same moon and stars.
Means...
That we are much closer than what we
actually, appear to be.*

She never would share her fears
or let you hear her cries.
She never would share her tears
that would fall from her gorgeous eyes.
It's been offered,
but never would she look for pity
or sympathy from anyone.
She would just smile like the morning sun
for absolutely everyone.

Her heart and her soul
carried the type of bravery,
the type of strength, and
the type of compassion.
dancing silent victories
under everything starry and dark,
conquering her beautiful world
in complete quietness.

-J. William-
Meet me under the same moon

I see your smile and that laugh too.
The stillness of your silence
around beautiful nature.
I can't help but to think,
do we really just exist
under the same sky, the same moon.
Seeing your wonderful energy
re-energized by love and peace,
and you surrounded by those
who love and care for you.
Just makes me wonder what kind of thoughts
are dancing through your mind right now.
I wish to know, but us being able to see
the same shooting star under the same night.
Makes me only wish, "to meet you one day of course,"
but most importantly to wish you
nothing but the best and for nothing to disturb your peace.
For you to keep glowing and growing
your beautiful soul with love and compassion,
with humility and empathy.
Wishing you find whatever it is you want and need
without obstacles and heartache.
Wishing that the world you dream of, will come true.
And who knows
hopefully maybe one day we shall meet,
under a same coffee menu.

-J. William-
Meet me under the same moon

255

Do you ever sometimes
feel too much,
that you are afraid
your heart will
swallow you whole.

-J. William-
Meet me under the same moon

I pray every night to the moon
and all its pretty little shining flowers.
To seed you with guidance, protection,
blessings, and so much love,
for you deserve it all and far more.

-J. William-
Meet me under the same moon

Our souls they fell in love,
way before us even knew
what love meant.

Now I know,
why I saw forever
when looking into your eyes.

Beautiful blue moon,
You are the muse to my writing,
and the study of
your romantic and passionate love.
Teaches the young heart of my soul
to express thought,
but like all great designs,
they are kept in secrecy.
Concealing all true intentions
from his one and only blue rose.
You know my name, but so does silence.
I wish it wasn't so, but like they say
"the night is still young"
and in every new night,
just know that I'll be looking at the moon,
carrying hope of maybe one day,
meeting you under the same moon.

Notes:

<u>Notes:</u>